MW00610937

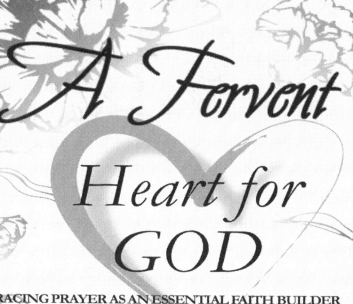

A Fervent
Heart for
GOD

EMBRACING PRAYER AS AN ESSENTIAL FAITH BUILDER
FOR A VICTORIOUS WALK WITH GOD

By Delia Wiggins

Lidan Publishing, LLC

Columbus, Georgia

Tidan Publishing LLC, P.O. Box 9482, Columbus, Georgia 31907, Tidanpublishingllc@gmail.com

Distributed by Tidan Publishing LLC
Cover Design & Illustrations by inspired by Tidan Publishing LLC & Jason Mahaffey of Southern City Art, LLC (southerncityart@gmail.com)

Scriptures marked as KJV are taken from the KING JAMES VERSION (KJV): KING JAMES VERSION, public domain.

Scriptures marked NIV are taken from the NEW INTERNATIONAL VERSION (NIV): Scripture taken from THE HOLY BIBLE, NEW INTERNATIONAL VERSION ®. Copyright© 1973, 1978, 1984, 2011 by Biblica, Inc.TM. Used by permission of Zondervan

Scriptures marked NKJV are taken from the NEW KING JAMES VERSION (NKJV): Scripture taken from the NEW KING JAMES VERSION®. Copyright© 1982 by Thomas Nelson, Inc. Used by permission. All rights reserved.

Scriptures marked TLB are taken from the THE LIVING BIBLE (TLB): Scripture taken from THE LIVING BIBLE copyright© 1971. Used by permission of Tyndale House Publishers, Inc., Carol Stream, Illinois 60188. All rights reserved.

Scriptures marked AMP are taken from the AMPLIFIED BIBLE (AMP): Scripture taken from the AMPLIFIED® BIBLE, Copyright © 1954, 1958, 1962, 1964, 1965, 1987 by the Lockman Foundation Used by Permission. (www.Lockman.org)

Scriptures marked NLT are taken from the HOLY BIBLE, NEW LIVING TRANSLATION (NLT): Scriptures taken from the HOLY BIBLE, NEW LIVING TRANSLATION, Copyright© 1996, 2004, 2007 by Tyndale House Foundation. Used by permission of Tyndale House Publishers, Inc., Carol Stream, Illinois 60188. All rights reserved. Used by permission.

Published 2021
Columbus, Georgia
Printed in the United States of America
ISBN 978-1-7353208-6-1
Library of Congress Control Number: Pending

Table of Contents

Dedication

Introduction   1

Chapter 1 - Prayer Defined   7

Chapter 2 - Activating Your Faith   15

Chapter 3 - Understanding Different Types of Prayer   21

Chapter 4 - Praise and Worship   31

Chapter 5 - The Foundation of Intercession   41

Chapter 6 - Knowing & Using Prayer as Your Spiritual Weapon   47

Chapter 7 - Understanding Praying in The Spirit   59

Chapter 8 - The Power of Prayer Confessions   71

Chapter 9 - Prayer Confessions for Your Life   77

My Inspirations   93

Acknowledgements & Thank Yous   99

About The Author   105

This book is dedicated to:

My Pastor and First Lady, Vince Allen and Beatrice Casiano Allen. Thank you for your leadership, mentorship, and your commitment to help the body of Christ to fulfill their purpose and reach their destiny. Because of your teaching, coaching, and encouragement. I have developed and continue to develop new levels of discipline, growth, and accomplishments. Thank you for your commitment to God and his people.

My mother, Alberta W. Holifield and my grandparents, Richmond & Delia Wiggins. Thank You Mother for carrying on the legacy of prayer, faith, and trust in God that was passed down from grandfather and grandmother. Thank you grandparents for the many Wednesday nights of family prayer, leading by example and teaching your lineage to follow God.

My children and grandchildren, I'm so very proud of you. Continue to press toward the Mark for the prize of the High Calling of God in Christ Jesus. Remember to **always** pray and don't faint. **Do not become weary in well doing,** for you will reap if you don't faint.

Introduction

My Beginning...
My Next Level...
My Now ...

Luke 18:1

*And he spake a parable unto them to this
end, that men ought always to pray, and not
to faint;*

My Beginning

I was born and raised in Sawyerville Alabama, which is mostly farmland. Our community consisted of one school, with both the elementary and middle schools together, a couple of convenience stores, a lot of farmland, and the families that live there. Our parents helped each other, shared with each other and helped raise each other's children. What I mean by that is, if you got out of line away from home, your parents were going to know about it by the time you got home. Quite different from today!!!

My grandparents were true farmers (entrepreneurs) so our family learned how to raise crops, cattle, horses, hogs, chickens and such. It was long hard work, but good earnest work. We also learned how to pray and trust God for our needs and the success of our endeavors each year, month, week, and each day.

During this time, we only met for service twice a month, the first and third Sunday of every month. So our grandparents taught us to always pray and trust God. I remember the Wednesday night prayer meetings that we would have over grandfather and grandmother's house every Wednesday. We would gather around in a big circle in the living room and the room next to the living room, because one room was not large enough to hold everyone. Grandfather and Grandmother would start the prayers and it would go from the elder to the youngest. Little did I know, these were seeds being planted in my heart and examples for me to live by and follow as I grew in life. The Word of God says to *"train up a child in the way he should go and when he is old, he will not depart from it."* (Proverbs 22:6)

So as I grew, so did the Word of God grow in me; my faith in God grew as well. My understanding of what all was taking place at the time was unfruitful, but God's Word is true and it works if we work it. So, praise God for my grandparents and parents working the Word and continuing to plant seeds in our hearts. In Mark 4:20 it says this, *"And these are they which are sown on good ground; such as hear the word, and receive it, and bring forth fruit, some thirtyfold, some sixty, and some an hundred."* I encourage every parent to sow the seeds of God's Word in the heart of your children, set the right examples before them, and train them up in the right way. My mother continued this Legacy. She would always talk to us about God's ability and encouraged us to keep our trust and confidence in the Lord. So at the age of 10, I wanted to know Jesus for myself. I shared my desire to know Jesus with my mother and she instructed me to ask God to forgive me for my sins and to come into my life as my Savior. I did, and my journey with the Lord began at that point. When living in "the country", there are not a lot of activities, places to go, or things to do, so my siblings and I would create our own games and activities. I also enjoyed reading the four gospel books, Matthew, Mark, Luke, John, and the book of Acts. The more I read, the more intrigued I became. Little did I know that the more I read, the more of the Word of God was being sowed in my heart and that Word came alive in me, causing me to crave more for God. My understanding was still not fruitful in how all of this worked, but I stayed the course.

I spent many days visualizing myself doing what Jesus did in the Books of Matthew, Mark, Luke, and John and what the apostles did in the book of Acts. The more I read the Word of God, the more I believed the Word of God. During my teen years, I became very ill. One morning I attempted to get up and start my day as usual and I could not stand up correctly without becoming very weak and dizzy. The doctor could not figure out what was causing the problem. I could not hold anything on my stomach. Everything I tried to eat or drink would return. No one knew what to do.

At this point, they gave my mother a prescription for me and told her to take me home and let me rest. Perhaps my body would return to normal functioning. Needless to say, I could not keep the pills down either. I remembered reading that Jesus healed them all. So I began to pray to God, "Daddy you are my healer, heal me." This went on for 7 days, but I continued to read, believe, and pray to God for my healing and on the seventh day, God healed me. I was able to eat some food, to drink some water, and stand up correctly without becoming weak, dizzy and having to lay back down. I experienced The Word of God in my physical body for myself! At that point, I knew God was a Healer. Life went on, but there was a yearning in my heart for more than what I was experiencing. However, I didn't know how to get there. During prayer I would say to God, "**Daddy there is more to you than I am experiencing right now and you are going to get me there.**" For the next four years of my life I held fast to believing that God was going to get me to the place where I could experience more of Him.

As I finished High School and signed up to serve my country for the next four years, I did not know it was all in God's plan to get me to the next place for growth, learning, and maturing in Him. He was working behind the scenes, putting everything and every person in place for my growth. He was preparing the answer to my heart's desire as I cried out to Him with such a simple prayer and confession. I didn't know I was confessing the Word as I prayed. Romans 4:17 says, *"...call those things **which be not** as though they were."* I was calling forth what was in my heart as I prayed, and God brought it to pass. We will talk more about the Simplicity of Prayer in Chapter 1, and The Power of Prayer Confessions in Chapter 8.

Holding on to God and getting to my next place of learning was not easy. Besides trying to interrupt my life with sickness, the devil also tried to perverse my mind, set up strongholds in my life, destroy my identity, and tried all kinds of distractions to pull me away from The Word. **But God, His Word, and the prayers of my ancestors** stopped the hand of the enemy from prevailing!

My Next Level

As I arrived at the next place God had prepared for my growth and learning, the stage was set and I began to learn about faith, the Holy Spirit, and His role in the life of a believer. I learned God desired to commune with me daily. He wanted me to spend time with Him and He with me. I submerged myself in everything I was learning, studying, and experiencing. Daddy and I were becoming one. My love for God grew more and more. I accepted the call to ministry and began to share the Good News of the Gospel with those I encountered each day.

My desire to help others experience what I was experiencing in God grew as well. I prayed with, prayed for, inspired, and encouraged people to give their life to God, or in many instances, return to God.

My Now

I am a lifetime learner, and God is yet teaching, training, developing, and maturing me in different areas of my life through different leaders, mentors, books, audios, and life itself. I am so grateful and thankful that I am becoming a better ambassador of Christ each day!

Chapter 1

Prayer Defined

Luke 18:1

*And he spake a parable unto them to this
end, that men ought always to pray, and not
to faint;*

Prayer is communication with God, sharing your heart and mind with God, and allowing time for God to share with you. God wants to commune or communicate with you, and this act involves more than one person. Therefore, prayer is a two-way conversation. With prayer you are not just talking to God, but it is also taking the time to listen and allow Him to speak to your heart. I love God's Word and I get excited when I read it! He knows our desires, our thoughts, our concerns, just examine 1 Pet 3:12, *"For the eyes of the Lord are on the righteous and his ears are attentive to their prayer, but the face of the Lord is against those who do evil. His Word promises that His ears are opened to the prayers of the righteous."* Who are the righteous? The sons and daughters of the King who have received Jesus, therefore, what Jesus did for us makes us righteous. In Romans 5:19 it states, *"For just as through the disobedience of the one man (Adam) the many were made sinners, so also through the obedience of the one man (Jesus) the many will be made righteous."* So you and I were made the righteousness of God through Jesus Christ! Amen. With that said, prayer is simply put, a conversation between you and God. God is a God of fellowship, and He desires to commune with us, to speak to our hearts and direct our paths according to His will for our lives. God speaks to us in several ways:

- Through His Word
- Through the Holy Spirit
- Through Prayer

We want to hear what God says, because He will answer our prayers according to His will for our lives. God's Word says in 1 Pet 5:7, *"Cast all your anxiety on him because he cares for you."* Our prayers to God are not a one way form of communication, but He promised us that if *we ask anything in His name, if we believe, we shall receive.* (Matthew 21:22)

Prayer is a "Faith Builder" and it also strengthens the inner man. The Word of God lets us know this in Jude 1:20, that *"when we pray in the spirit, we are built up in our most holy faith."* I have a chapter dedicated to praying in the spirit. When we pray, we are building up our faith so that we can begin to see God bring those things we are praying for to pass! Therefore, when God answers our prayers, it builds our faith and increases our confidence in Him. As you trust God more, it will cause you to pray more.

The Simplicity of Prayer

A lot of people believe that prayer is something difficult, or that only pastors, or ministers can pray. Some feel unqualified to pray, maybe you are new in Christ and you are concerned that you don't sound like this person or that person. Lastly, maybe you believe that you are praying and God does not hear you. If you fall into any of these categories, you will be overjoyed to know that none of the above scenarios are true. God wants you to come to Him just as you are, with an open heart and a willing spirit. He wants you to come to Him just like a child comes to a parent. Just like our parents, He wants to take care of us, protect us because He loves us so much.

God wants a relationship with us, interaction, true intimacy with us. He lets us know this over and over in His Word of His desire to communicate. He says the following:

Jeremiah 33:3 - "Call to Me, and I will answer you, and show you great and mighty things, which you do not know."

Psalm 50:15 - "and call on me in the day of trouble; I will deliver you, and you will honor me.

Psalm 91:16. "With long life will I satisfy him, and shew him my salvation."

James 4:8 - "Draw near to God, and he will draw near to you..."

Just like a relationship here on earth, as we spend time with people and begin to talk to them more and more, we begin to <u>know</u> them better. However, without consistent and meaningful communication with that person, that transformation does not happen. The same can be said of your relationship with God through prayer. There should be a transformation of your prayer life with God, and this happens through spending time with God through prayer and reading His Word. God wants to know all about our cares and concerns. In 1 Thessalonians 5:17, God tells us to pray without ceasing, in other words, pray continually. This is the will of God for our lives because as we pray to God and seek His face, in the process we are getting to know Him, His ways, and His Word.

God desires that we come to Him with boldness and confidence to experience His grace and mercy in our time of need. (Hebrews 4:16)   He is a loving Father willing, ready, and able to help all of His children regardless of the circumstances. He will forgive us of our sins if we confess our faults, our shortcomings, and when we miss the mark. He is faithful and just to forgive us and cleanse us from all unrighteousness. (1 John 1:9)   I pray that you will start spending time communing with your Father because He desires to spend time with you.

Why Should We Pray?

According to Philippians 4:6, the Word of God lets us know that prayer is how we make our requests known to God. Does God know our thoughts before we even think them, yes He does! (Psalm 139:1-5).   However, remember that God also desires fellowship with his children, therefore He wants us to come to Him. God wants a relationship with us, a two-way relationship. He has so much in store for us if we can just trust Him.

When we petition God in prayer, just as you would give to your own children when they ask of you, we can have full confidence that we shall have whatever we ask of God, according to His will. Mark 11:24 states, *"And* **whatever you ask in prayer, you** *will receive, if* **you** *have faith." Therefore* **I** *tell* **you**, **whatever you ask in prayer,** *believe that* **you** *have received it, and it will be yours."* We know that He hears us, and because we know that He hears us, we know that we can have it, Amen!

The Word of God states in Luke 18:1, *"that we should always pray and not faint."* This means God understood that the flesh can get weary. However, He promises if we pray and not faint that His Word will strengthen us! His Word will cause us not to become weary in our mind, nor will we give up, cave in or quit. The enemy is always sending fiery darts to the mind to get us distracted from the Word so we will become weary. We can overcome all his strategies and stand firm in prayer, which will also keep us from yielding to temptation. (Matthew 26:41) According to Psalm 119:11, we *"hide His Word in our heart so we may not sin against Him."*

Prayer is an essential and critical part to our Christian walk. So as we are praying to God and seeking His face, it causes us to become strong in the Lord and in the power of His might. As we are praying the Word of God, that Word is also getting in our heart. We will overcome all the trials, the tests, and the temptations because we exercise our faith through prayer and the Word of God.

God's Word explains what the prayer of faith can do in James 5:14-15. It reads, *"Is any sick among you? let him call for the elders of the church; and let them pray over him, anointing him with oil in the name of the Lord: And **the prayer of faith shall save the sick**, and the Lord **shall** raise him up; and if he have committed sins, they **shall** be forgiven him."*

I pray that this book will inspire you to establish or enhance your prayer life. Building a trusting relationship with Him will result in you walking step by step with God, and living life more abundantly because of your powerful prayer life!

Chapter 2

Activating Your Faith

Luke 18:1

And he spake a parable unto them to this end, that men ought always to pray, and not to faint;

When we get ready to drive a car, we have the key that unlocks the door; we sit down in the car and position ourselves to drive, then we put the key in the ignition, we turn it on, and when all is well that car starts, and we then travel to our next destination. Makes sense, right? In that same way when we pray, we have our keys, which is God's Word, we put them in the "ignition", which is our prayers ignited and activated by faith, and we travel to our next destination. Line upon line, precept upon precept, faith to faith, and glory to glory.

We need faith to activate the keys of God's Word in our lives. *In Matthew 11:24 it reads, "Therefore I say unto you, What things soever ye desire, **when ye pray, <u>believe</u> <u>that ye receive them</u>,** and ye shall have them."* So we must use our prayer life to activate our faith and apply the Word of God. Hebrews 11:6 says *"without faith it is impossible to please God."* Romans 10:17 also tells us that *"faith comes by hearing and hearing the Word of God."* That means hearing and hearing, and consistently hearing the Word of God. How do we do that?

We hear the Word through reading the Word, and God will speak to us.
We hear the Word through fellowship with other believers.
We hear the Word from our pastor and ministers.

But when we pray the Word of God, and we mix it with our faith we can set an expectation that is going to work just like when you put that key in your car ignition and expect it to start.

As I referenced in chapter 1, prayer is a "faith builder," meaning you build upon your faith every time you pray, and as your faith grows, your expectations grow as well because you see the manifestation of the Word of God. You may start by only saying a few sentences, but your spirit-man will help you build upon those few sentences and scriptures daily. As you read the Word and you fill yourself up with the Word, you will find the Word flowing out of you effortlessly and effectively. An important fact to note here, do not worry about trying to pray like everyone else. Someone may pray and all you hear is scriptures, others may mix scriptures in with declarations and confessions. God will give you what to pray for and it will be pleasing to God because it's from your heart. As Christians, I believe we mess ourselves up and get in our own way because we're so concerned about how others are praying. My advice to you would be to pray in a way that is pleasing to God, seek to please Him, and your prayer life will be effective. Your prayers are personal and special to God, seek His face, and you will find your intimacy with Him is time well spent, that you dare not miss!

Activating your faith is not always easy. Hebrews 11:1 makes it clear what having "now faith" is, *"Now faith is the substance of things hoped for, the evidence of things not seen."* We want **"NOW"** faith to activate a **"LATER"** blessing. That can be difficult to process, but God's Word tells us that *"those that believe, but have not yet seen are blessed!"* (John 20:29). So we want to be among those blessed believers because we are putting our hope, expectations, and trust in God! Amen. We can pray the prayer of faith and God will answer according to our faith. Jesus affirms this several times throughout His ministry. He said, *"be it unto them according to your faith."* (Matthew 9:29) So we can pray the prayer of faith to receive what we desire from the Lord.

We can believe God for anything because we have seen our faith in action. Think about all the things that God has done for you, and if He did it before, He can and will do it again! He surely loves us without limits, and God does things like no one else can do. Not only does He give you what you need, but He does so in such a way that no one else could have done it. He is the Great I AM! Hallelujah!

Sometimes I speak to God about things that only He and I know about. When those specific things come to fruition, I know without a doubt that God's Word is in action. It is the God of my life whom I've been trusting for so long, the on-time God, the limitless and gracious God, the only wise and omniscient God, it's Him working it out on my behalf, just for me!

In order to increase the expectation that you have for Him,

you must activate your faith. If you trust God will hear and answer your prayers, you must trust Him in the little things and the great things in your life. We have the keys, the map, the blueprints, and they are all in God's Word! We serve a God who has given us everything to thrive, grow, and to live a successful and abundant spirit-filled life! It's just up to us to pray His Word, have faith enough to activate those prayers. All we have to do is wait on the Lord and have full expectation, knowing He shall bring it to pass. Activate your faith today! Amen.

Chapter 3

Understanding Different Types of Prayer

Luke 18:1

And he spake a parable unto them to this end, that men ought always to pray, and not to faint;

Let's go a step further now that we have talked about the importance of prayer and why we should pray. This chapter will focus on understanding different types of prayers. I have dedicated entire chapters to Praise and Worship, the Prayer of Confession, and the Foundation of Intercession because these three areas need their own chapter.

THE PRAYER OF AGREEMENT OR CORPORATE PRAYER

The prayer of agreement or corporate prayer is described in the book of Matthew 18:19. The Word of God states, *"Again I say unto you, That if two of you shall agree on earth as touching any thing that they shall ask, it shall be done for them of my Father which is in heaven."* So we can operate in the prayer of agreement, whether this is done corporately, or with two individuals, God is in the midst. One thing that we should remember is that whether there are two or several individuals, God cannot and will not answer your prayers for someone else <u>against their will.</u> God does not go against someone's will, He is a gentleman. So we have to come in agreement <u>with the person</u> that we are a praying for, or for their situation so that we can pray in agreement with <u>their will.</u> The prayer of faith in James 5:14-16 states *"Is anyone among you sick? Let him call for the elders of the church, and let them pray over him, anointing him with oil in the name of the Lord. And the prayer of faith will save the sick, and the Lord will raise him up. And if he has committed sins, he will be forgiven. Confess your trespasses to one another, and pray for one another, that you may be healed. The effective, fervent prayer of a righteous man avails much."*

An example of the power of prayer is found in the book of Acts 12:1-17, and it reads *"now about that time Herod the king stretched forth his hand to vex certain of the church and he killed James the brother of John with a sword. And because he saw it pleased the Jews he proceeded further to take Peter also (then were the days of unleavened bread). And when he had apprehended him, he put him in prison, and delivered him to four quaternions of soldiers to keep him; intending after Easter to bring him forth to the people. And when Herod would have brought him forth, the same night Peter was sleeping between two soldiers, bound with two chains: and the keepers before the door kept the prison. And, behold, the angel of the Lord came upon him, and a light shined in the prison: and he smote Peter on the side, and raised him up, saying, Arise up quickly. And his chains fell off from his hands. And the angel said unto him, Gird thyself, and bind on thy sandals. And so he did. And he saith unto him, Cast thy garment about thee, and follow me. And he went out, and followed him; and wist not that it was true which was done by the angel; but thought he saw a vision. When they were past the first and the second ward, they came unto the iron gate that leadeth unto the city; which opened to them of his own accord: and they went out, and passed on through one street; and forthwith the angel departed from him. And when Peter had come to himself, he said, Now I know of a surety, that the Lord hath sent his angel, and hath delivered me out of the hand of Herod, and from all the expectation of the people of the Jews. And when he had considered the thing, he came to the house of Mary the mother of John, whose surname was Mark;* **where many were gathered together praying.** *And as Peter knocked at the door of the gate, a damsel came to hearken, named Rhoda. And when she knew Peter's voice, she opened not the gate for gladness, but ran in, and told how Peter stood before the gate. And they said unto her, Thou art mad. But she constantly affirmed that it was even so. Then said they, It is his angel. But Peter continued knocking: and when they had opened the door, and saw him, they were astonished. But he, beckoning unto them with the hand to hold their peace, declared unto them how the Lord had brought him out of the prison. And he said, Go shew these things unto James, and to the brethren. And he departed, and went into another place."*

You see how this is a prime example of the power of corporate prayer? Prayer is a very powerful weapon and God has given believers that ability through the Word of God. His Word tells us that *"One can put a thousand to flight, and two can put ten thousand to flight"* (Deuteronomy 32:30). We can see how God multiplies when there is unity, and what can happen when two people stand on the Word of God and do warfare. If warfare can put ten thousand demonic spirits to flight, then what can a whole Body of Christ do? It is amazing what the power of prayer can do! I want to encourage every believer to utilize the power and the authority that Father God has given each one of us.

THE PRAYER OF FAITH

God answers prayers but it is our faith that brings those answers out of the spirit realm into the physical realm. In the Book of Matthew the 9th chapter, beginning at verse 1, God's Word explains that Jesus stepped into a boat, crossed over and came to His own town. Some men brought to Him a paralyzed man, lying on a mat. When Jesus saw **their faith,** He said to the man, *"Take heart, son; your sins are forgiven."* The man was made whole, but Jesus said it was according to **their faith.** So it was Jesus' power that healed the people, but He accredited **their faith** with being the catalyst. In Mark 11:24 it says *"Therefore I tell you, whatever you ask for **in prayer, believe** that you have received it, and it will be yours."*

So it is when we pray and believe that we receive it, and then we will have it. Remember, when we pray in faith God immediately gives the answer to our prayers in the spirit realm, but in the natural realm it may take time for the answer to manifest itself. An example of this is found in Daniel 10:12-13 where a messenger of the Lord spoke to Daniel in a vision and said, *"Do not be afraid, Daniel. Since **the first day** that you set your mind to gain understanding and to humble yourself before your God, your words were heard, and I have come in response to them. But the prince of the Persian kingdom resisted me for 21 days. Then Michael, one of the chief princes, came to help me, because I was detained there with the king of Persia."* Now in this particular passage of scripture, the messenger of the Lord said the **very first day** that Daniel's prayers were heard and the answer was sent. However, the messenger went into battle with the enemy because he was trying to intercept, or to keep the answer that Daniel needed from reaching him. So that was warfare going on in order for Daniel to get his answer. Daniel's answer was sent the **very first day.** We have to exercise faith and patience in order to receive the answer in the natural--or earth realm when we are praying the prayer of faith.

PRAYER AND SUPPLICATION WITH THANKSGIVING

Philippians 4:6 says *"be anxious or be careful for nothing but in everything by prayer and supplication with Thanksgiving let your requests be made known to God."* So we can avoid anxiety simply by taking our requests to God in prayer with thanksgiving. Now thanksgiving causes us to focus on what God has done, and who He is. We notice that scriptures do not indicate when we will receive results of our prayer, neither does it give us a time frame of when the answered prayers will appear. What we have to do is believe God, and by faith know that we have the petition that we have asked of him. It's kind of like when you plant a seed in the ground, you cannot see what's taking place under the ground with the seed and the soil, but you know that the seed and the soil are at work. Over time we will see the results of the seed in the soil that was at work under the ground. Eventually you will begin to see the plant spring up above the ground. It is the same way with how our prayer and faith works. In Mark 4:26-30 it says, *"And he said, So is the kingdom of God, as if a man should cast seed into the ground;*

And should sleep, and rise night and day, and the seed should spring and grow up, he knoweth not how. For the earth bringeth forth fruit of herself; first the blade, then the ear, after that the full corn in the ear. But when the fruit is brought forth, immediately he putteth in the sickle, because the harvest is come. And he said, Whereunto shall we liken the kingdom of God? or with what comparison shall we compare it?" God is working behind the scenes as we hold fast to His Word! Amen.

THE PRAYER OF CONSECRATION & DEDICATION

The prayer of consecration and dedication consists of setting aside time for ourselves, or setting ourselves apart to follow God's will. Jesus was speaking to Peter, James, and John, in the book of

Luke 22:41-42 states, *"And He was withdrawn from them about a stone's throw, and He knelt down and prayed, saying, "Father, if it is Your will, take this cup away from Me; nevertheless not My will, but Yours, be done."* **In this particular scripture, Jesus was actually consecrating and dedicating Himself completely to His Father, so He could carry out His Father's will.** In the same way, we can dedicate and consecrate ourselves to the Father when we have two or more Godly alternatives before us, and we are not getting a clear sense at that time about which option God wants us to take. So we can pray this prayer and come before the Lord to get clarity on what direction we need to take. We can also use this prayer of consecration and dedication if we just want to draw closer to the Lord. This way, our hearing can be more keen and we will gain the fellowship we desire and need from our Father.

THE PRAYER OF BINDING AND LOOSING

In the prayer of binding and loosing Matthew 18:18-19 says *"Truly I tell you, whatever you bind on earth will be bound in heaven, and whatever you loose on earth will be loosed in heaven. Again, truly I tell you that if two of you on earth agree about anything they ask for, it will be done for them by my Father in heaven."* I want you to know that this is a part of our covenant right as a believer, but we must first bind and loose here on earth before it will be done in heaven. We can exercise our covenant right of power and authority that we have been given by God here on earth by binding what needs to be bound, and loosing what needs to be loosed. But, this prayer only works in line with God's Word, His will, and His law. We can't just bind and loose any and everything, it has to be according to the Word of God. It is not based on what we want or what we desire, you can bind foul spirits that are at work in people's lives, or you can loose angelic spirits to work on behalf of others according to what God has promised in His Word.

THE PRAYER OF COMMITMENT

The prayer of commitment in Psalm 37:5-6 says *"commit your way to the Lord trust also in him and He shall bring it to pass. He shall bring forth your righteousness as the light, and your justice as the Noonday."* We can also pray the prayer of commitment as shown in 1 Pet 5:6-7 which says, *"Therefore humble yourself under the mighty hand of God that he may exalt you in due time casting all your cares upon Him for He cares for you."* The prayer of commitment involves committing ourselves to the Lord and committing our ways to the Lord, so that He can establish our thoughts and our plans. He can bring them to pass, He can order our steps in the direction that we need to go, and in the decisions we need to make when we pray the prayer of commitment.

The examples that I have highlighted for you are just enough to help you understand what God has placed in His Word regarding the different types of prayer. Please know that there are several more and it is my prayer that you continue to seek the scriptures for yourself to gain additional knowledge and understanding. You will also find specific confessions in Chapter 9.

Chapter 4

Praise & Worship

Luke 18:1

And he spake a parable unto them to this end, that men ought always to pray, and not to faint;

The ministry of Praise and Worship is when you take the time to focus on God. This is a time to express praise and admiration for whom He is to you. We want to tell God we love Him, adore Him, and appreciate Him for who He is.

I wanted to highlight praise and worship separately because it truly deserves an important emphasis. When we look at Matthew 6:9-13 , the 'model prayer', "*After this manner therefore pray ye: Our Father which art in heaven, Hallowed be thy name. Thy kingdom come, Thy will be done on earth, as it is in heaven. Give us this day our daily bread. And forgive us our debts, as we forgive our debtors. And lead us not into temptation, but deliver us from evil: For thine is the kingdom, and the power, and the glory, forever. Amen.*" In what we call 'The Lord's Prayer', God starts us off with " hallowed be thy name." When you review this same passage of scripture in the Amplified Bible, the word **hallow** means to set apart, keep and treat as holy, and to revere. So within the act of prayer, we are to ensure that we reverence God and remember He is holy, and we are praying to our Father. When I was in the military, there were certain customs and courtesies that we rendered to those of superior rank or grade. Some required a salute when we were outside, others may have required the room to stand upon their entry, we were paying respect to that "superior" officer's rank. Likewise, but so much more with God, when we pray, we hallow His name, which is honoring, reverencing, and paying holy respect to the King of Kings and The Lord of Lords. Amen.

Worship focuses on who God is, and praise expresses admiration for who He is to you. In Luke 18:35-43, there was a young man needed to receive his sight, *"As Jesus approached Jericho, a blind man was sitting by the roadside begging. When he heard the crowd going by, he asked what was happening. They told him, "Jesus of Nazareth is passing by." He called out, "Jesus, Son of David, have mercy on me!" Those who led the way rebuked him and told him to be quiet, but he shouted all the more, "Son of David, have mercy on me!" Jesus stopped and ordered the man to be brought to him. When he came near, Jesus asked him, "What do you want me to do for you?" "Lord, I want to see," he replied. Jesus said to him,* **"Receive your sight; your faith has healed you."** *Immediately he received his sight and followed Jesus, praising God. When all the people saw it, they also praised God."*

In Luke 2:20, we see an example of the shepherds going to see the child Jesus that was born to be King, *"The shepherds returned, glorifying and praising God for all the things they had heard and seen, which were just as they had been told."* This is basically a prayer of praise and worship. You are exalting God and you are glorifying God through prayer, praise and worship. You are magnifying Him for who He is and what He is to you as an individual.

Worship, as I stated above, is focusing on who God is. Worship is an experience that we want to enter into repeatedly with God. It is here we are able to really begin to focus on "who" God is, **not what He can do for us**, but who He is to us, it is amazing! The refreshing and enlightenment that comes from worshipping God is not manufactured, but led by The Holy Spirit. It is in our worship time with God that we can feel the essence of His unconditional love for us. We can never really fully conceive God's love for His children, it is immeasurable and never-ending. God's love is like no other love you will experience in your lifetime. God is our heavenly Father, and just like our earthly father, He loves when our focus is on Him. He loves when we acknowledge Him, consult Him, and talk with Him. Without God, there would be no you or I. He has created everything, and holds all power in His hands. Our ancestors worshipped God, throughout the scriptures the importance of worshipping God was displayed and conveyed over and over again. John 4:24 tells us that *"God is spirit, and his worshipers must worship in Spirit and in truth."* Our worship time with God should be revered and cherished as a supernatural time with our sovereign God.

Praise and Worship is also a spiritual weapon when you look at 2 Chronicles 20:20-25, God shows us that praise and worship was used as a spiritual weapon when he gave King Jehoshaphat instructions when they were facing the battle against the enemy. It reads, *"Early in the morning they left for the Desert of Tekoa. As they set out, Jehoshaphat stood and said, "Listen to me, Judah and people of Jerusalem! Have faith in the Lord your God and you will be upheld; have faith in his prophets and you will be successful." After consulting the people, Jehoshaphat appointed men to sing to the Lord and to praise him for the splendor of his holiness as they went out at the head of the army, saying:*

"Give thanks to the Lord, for his love endures forever."

As they began to sing and praise, the Lord set ambushes against the men of Ammon and Moab and Mount Seir who were invading Judah, and they were defeated. The Ammonites and Moabites rose up against the men from Mount Seir to destroy and annihilate them. After they finished slaughtering the men from Seir, they helped to destroy one another. When the men of Judah came to the place that overlooks the desert and looked toward the vast army, they saw only dead bodies lying on the ground; no one had escaped. So Jehoshaphat and his men went to carry off their plunder, and they found among them a great amount of equipment and clothing and also articles of value—more than they could take away. There was so much plunder that it took three days to collect it."

So you see praise and worship is a weapon against the enemy so as we praise God, and we worship the Lord, then God is able to confuse the enemy. In the instance above, He was able to set up ambushes against the enemy which caused the enemy to take his own self out, glory be to God!

Here are a few scriptures to meditate on when you are worshipping God for who He is:

Do not worship any other god, for the Lord, whose name is Jealous, is a jealous God. (Exodus 34:14)

Rather, worship the Lord your God; it is he who will deliver you from the hand of all your enemies. (2 Kings 17:39)

*Worship the Lord your God, and his blessing will be on your food and water. (*Exodus 23:25)

Bless the Lord, O my soul, and forget not all his benefits: Who forgiveth all thine iniquities; who healeth all thy diseases; Who redeemeth thy life from destruction; who crowneth thee with lovingkindness and tender mercies; Who satisfieth thy mouth with good things; so that thy youth is renewed like the eagle's. (Psalm 103:1-5)

But may the righteous be glad and rejoice before God; may they be happy and joyful. Sing to God, sing in praise of his name, extol him who rides on the clouds; rejoice before him—his name is the Lord.

A father to the fatherless, a defender of widows, is God in his holy dwelling. God sets the lonely in families, he leads out the prisoners with singing; but the rebellious live in a sun-scorched land. (Psalm 68:3-6)

Worship is very important to God, and we must worship God in our giving, our living, with our hearts, and with our lives. Practice worshiping God and watch Him perform the supernatural just for you because He loves when we truly worship Him. Equally as important is our praise. We praise God for who He is to us, and for what He has done for us.

Praise is so powerful, and most essential to our Christian journey. If you review Psalm 22:3, it tells us that God inhabits the praise of His people, so we want to please God and abide in Him. It reads, *"But thou art holy, O thou that inhabitest the praises of Israel."* We surely want God to abide where we are and we want Him to be pleased with our offering. I have to imagine that just as we offer a gift to someone and they are happy and appreciative, glowing with excitement, we want our God to be pleased in that same way -- happy, excited, and receptive. We want Him to hear and receive our praise as an offering unto Him. Praise is another way to honor and esteem God. Here are some scriptures to meditate on regarding our praise to God:

I give you thanks, O Lord, with all my heart; I will sing your praises before the gods. (Psalm 138:1)

I will give thanks to the Lord because of his righteousness; I will sing the praises of the name of the Lord Most High. (Psalm 7:17)

Sing to the Lord with grateful praise; make music to our God on the harp. (Psalm 147:7)

Praise the Lord. Praise the Lord, you his servants; praise the name of the Lord. Let the name of the Lord be praised, both now and forevermore. From the rising of the sun to the place where it sets, the name of the Lord is to be praised. (Psalm 113:1-3)

Enter his gates with thanksgiving and his courts with praise; give thanks to him and praise his name. For the Lord is good and his love endures forever; his faithfulness continues through all generations. (Psalm 100:4-5)

I will praise God's name in song and glorify him with thanksgiving. (Psalm 69:30)

Praise the Lord. Give thanks to the Lord, for he is good; his love endures forever. (Psalm 106:1)

Whether you are engaged in praise, worship, or both, know that God is looking forward to communing and connecting with you. You may participate corporately, or individually, but create an atmosphere to praise and worship the Lord and you will see the supernatural show up in your life on even greater levels. Amen!

David declares in Psalm 34:1, "*I will bless the Lord at **all times**: his praise shall continually be in my mouth.*" So basically what this verse is saying is that I will praise God at all times! I will praise Him no matter what happens, or no matter what does not happen, I will praise God! Then verse 2 goes on to say, "*My soul shall make her boast in the Lord: the humble shall hear thereof, and be glad.*" In other words, David is saying, I will brag on my Daddy, I will boast in Him, I will tell everyone about how good my God is! Verse 3 continues with "*O magnify the Lord with me, and let us exalt his name together.*" The word **magnify** means to make large. We know that we can't make God larger, but we can magnify His name, lift His name, and make His name large with our praise. Now let me ask you this question. Have you ever sought the Lord and He heard your cry, delivered you, and saved you? If so, then you have a reason to magnify the Lord, to brag on Him, to boast on Him, you have a reason because God is so good to us!!!! No matter what happens, praise ye The Lord!!!

Chapter 5

The Foundation of Intercession

Luke 18:1

And he spake a parable unto them to this end, that men ought always to pray, and not to faint;

The prayer of intercession involves praying for others, essentially you are interested in acting on behalf of someone else through prayer. This includes praying for the Body of Christ, our spiritual leaders, pastors, teachers, prophets, evangelists, our president and cabinet, for our government officials, and for those in authority. In 1 Timothy 2:1-4, it states *"I exhort therefore, that, first of all, supplications, prayers, intercessions, and giving of thanks, be made for all men; For kings, and for all that are in authority; that we may lead a quiet and peaceable life in all godliness and honesty. For this is good and acceptable in the sight of God our Saviour; Who will have all men to be saved, and to come unto the knowledge of the truth."* In Ephesians 1:15-18 it says, *"Therefore I also, after I heard of your faith in the Lord Jesus and your love for all the saints, do not cease to give thanks for you, making mention of you in my prayers: that the God of our Lord Jesus Christ, the Father of glory, may give to you the spirit of wisdom and revelation in the knowledge of Him, the eyes of your understanding being enlightened; that you may know what is the hope of His calling, what are the riches of the glory of His inheritance in the saints."* In this passage, Paul explains he will pray and intercede on behalf of the Saints.

So the prayer of intercession is praying on behalf of someone else so they may receive their breakthrough, the answer, or wisdom from God. When intercession becomes your custom, because you see the hand of God, you will find yourself praying for people all of the time. That is what God wants us to do, pray for one another and He especially wants us to pray for those that are lost. God desires that everyone come into His Kingdom and have an abundant life on earth. When I think about salvation, I'm always reminded that someone prayed for me. That's what we have to remember when we lost our way, or lived our lives in ways that may not have been pleasing to God, we have to remember someone prayed for us. In my case I know it was what I call my "Legacy," my grandparents, my mother, my aunts, and my family, they prayed for me. Someone prayed for you, too. I don't know who it was, there were many I am sure, but I know that as you read this you are thanking God for them. There is nothing like the feeling of being used by God for the betterment of someone else. To be used in the plan of God for someone's life is an honor and a privilege. This is what intercession is all about. Whether you are praying for someone who can't pray for themselves or doesn't know how to pray, or you are praying for someone because you know a situation needs prayer. No matter what the reason, you are a vessel of God using your gift of intercession to bring about a blessed change in someone's life. This alone is an honor.

I love to see God's Word in action. Through intercessory prayer, I witness many, many situations being turned around. One thing to remember, when someone asks you to pray for them, if you can do it at that moment, do it! We all get busy and, more importantly, we don't understand the timeliness attached to the prayer request. We don't know what is going on in the spiritual realm concerning that person's situation. What we know is the timing of God, which is always right on time! Therefore, when someone asks you to pray, you can put God's Word out in the atmosphere quickly and let it begin to operate immediately in Jesus name. You can pray for a hedge of protection around that person, their family, and their situation. Hebrews 4:12 states, *"For the word of God is living and powerful, and sharper than any two-edged sword, piercing even to the division of soul and spirit, and of joints and marrow, and is a discerner of the thoughts and intents of the heart."* It is our charge to activate our faith, pray God's Word, and watch God work it out! I believe it is also very comforting and builds the faith of the one that asked you to pray when you move immediately to pray for them versus waiting. When they are a part of what you are praying for, and they hear your prayers, it gives them faith and hope for the situation. Intercessory prayer will allow you to see firsthand God's Word in action. I challenge any of you to be a part of the intercessory prayer team at your church, linking up with people of like precious faith and watching God's Word manifest continuously in the lives of God's people. It has been my experience with intercessory prayer that as I pray for others and their needs, God takes care of my needs.

Remember, God knows what we need before we even ask. (Matthew 6:8) What better way to exemplify God's love than to pray for the needs of His people, even when they cannot pray for themselves.

Chapter 6

Knowing & Using Prayer As Your Spiritual Weapon

Luke 18:1

And he spake a parable unto them to this end, that men ought always to pray, and not to faint;

Exercise your right to use your spiritual weapons. That is why I want to have a vibrant prayer life because of what prayer can do not only in my own life, but in the lives of others. God commands us to pray for all men, and to pray for all saints, so we want to utilize the weapon that God has given each and every one of us that believes. The Word of God lets us know that Jesus has already defeated Satan and overcame the world. In Colossians 2:15, *"and having spoiled principalities and power he made a show of them openly triumphing over them in it."* So Jesus has already overcome satan and all of his forces. In John 16:33, Jesus states *"I have told you these things, so that in me you may have peace. In this world you will have trouble. But take heart! I have overcome the world."* There are many passages of scripture that confirm to us how Jesus defeated satan, Hallelujah! Because Jesus did, we can also. Multiple times in God's Word we are reminded not to be dismayed or disappointed about the end result, because in the end, WE WIN!

God has given us many spiritual weapons, for that reason it is very important that every believer understands and uses their spiritual weapons, especially the weapon of prayer. In the book of Ephesians Chapter 6, God tells us a lot about our weapons. We do not fight a natural fight but it is <u>spiritual warfare</u>. We are also taught that along with these spiritual weapons, we are to fight the good fight of faith. In the book of 1 Tim 6:12, it reads, *"Fight the good fight of the faith. Take hold of the eternal life to which you were called when you made your good confession in the presence of many witnesses."* The only fight that we should be fighting is the good fight, so when we fight it's not a natural fight but a spiritual fight. We should hold fast to the Word of God which enables us to be victorious in that spiritual fight, because this fight has already been won by Jesus. Also, God reminded us four times that the *"just shall live by faith,"* why did He repeat this four times? I believe that He wanted us to understand clearly that faith will equip us for every battle. Review these scriptures:

Habakkuk 2:4	*"...but the just shall live by his faith."*
Galatians 3:11	*"But that no one is justified by the law in the sight of God it is evident, for "the just shall live by faith."*
Hebrews 10:38	*"Now the just shall live by faith..."*
Romans 1:17	*"For therein is the righteousness of God revealed from faith to faith: as it is written, The just shall live by faith."*

We must know what our spiritual weapons are so we can use them to fight the good fight of faith when we need to wage war. Paul states in 1 Timothy 1:18-19, *"Timothy, my son, here are my instructions for you, based on the prophetic words spoken about you earlier. May they help you fight well in the Lord's battles. Cling to your faith in Christ, and keep your conscience clear. For some people deliberately violated their consciences; as a result, their faith has been shipwrecked."* So we want to fight the good fight of faith keeping our conscience clear.

Let's see what God says about our warfare in 2 Corinthians 10:3-5, *"For though we walk in the flesh, we do not war after the flesh: For the weapons of our warfare are not carnal, but mighty through God to the pulling down of strong holds; Casting down imaginations, and every high thing that exalteth itself against the knowledge of God, and bringing into captivity every thought to the obedience of Christ."* God also tells us through the scriptures that warfare begins in our mind, so we have to renew our mind in order to wage good warfare against the enemy. We know that the enemy will send different fiery darts to the mind, but the Word of God lets us know that we have to renew our mind. In Romans 12:2 it states, *"And be not conformed to this world: but be ye transformed by the renewing of your mind, that ye may prove what is that good, and acceptable, and perfect, will of God."* This scripture is telling us not to fashion ourselves after this world, but to be changed and transformed by renewing our mind. We do this by reading, praying, confessing, and doing the Word of God which will cause us to operate in the mind of Christ.

God has given us spiritual weapons to war with, and they are found in Ephesians Chapter 6. This entire chapter of Ephesians is noteworthy, but I will begin at Ephesians 6:10-18, and it reads as follows: *"Finally, my brethren, be strong in the Lord and in the power of His might. Put on the whole armor of God, that you may be able to stand against the wiles of the devil. **For we do not wrestle against flesh and blood**, but against principalities, against powers, against the rulers of the darkness of this age, against spiritual hosts of wickedness in the heavenly places. Therefore take up the whole armor of God, that you may be able to withstand in the evil day, and having done all, to stand. Stand therefore, **having girded your waist with truth,** having put on the **breastplate of righteousness, and having shod your feet with the preparation of the gospel of peace;** above all, taking the **shield of faith** with which you will be able to quench all the fiery darts of the wicked one. And take the **helmet of salvation,** and the **sword of the Spirit, which is the word of God; praying always** with all prayer and supplication in the Spirit, being watchful to this end with all perseverance and supplication for all the saints. "* This list given in Ephesians lets us know that we can't do anything in our own power, but we must do it in the strength of the Lord.

This is why we have to renew our carnal mind, which can only be done through the Word of God. This is how we operate with the mind of Christ. Here are our weapons, and then I will break each of them down:

Spiritual Weapon	Scripture Reference
Loins girded with truth	Ephesians 6:14
Breastplate of Righteousness	Ephesians 6:14
Feet prepared with the gospel of peace	Ephesians 6:15
Shield of Faith	Ephesians 6:16
Helmet of Salvation	Ephesians 6:17
Sword of The Spirit/The Word of God	Ephesians 6:17
Prayer	Ephesians 6:18
The Blood of Jesus	Revelation 12:11
The Name of Jesus	Philippians 2:9-11

We should put this armor of God on and keep it on, so in the spiritual realm we are protected. We know that the Word says *"no weapon it's formed against us shall prosper"* (Isaiah 54:17), and God also gives us every spiritual weapon that we need to wage warfare spiritually and come out victorious. The devil is going to do his job, he's going to send weapons and missiles to our mind, so we have to have the mind of Christ and the helmet of salvation to defeat those weapons.

Weapons can come in the form of doubt, lack, fear, and less than, but we are victorious when our mind is renewed through the

Word of God. Verse 12 tells us that our battle is spiritual, not flesh and blood. Therefore, we are to take on the whole armor of God, using every piece of equipment, not some of it but all of it, to stand against the enemy in the evil days.

Now let's break down this equipment that God has given us. First, scripture instructs that our **loins be girded about with truth,** some refer to this as our "buckler," as it is like a belt around our waist so we have it on all of the time. In Psalm 91:4 it states in part, *"His truth shall be your shield and buckler."* This indicates that the truth of God's Word is what we want to feed ourselves with as a part of the deity of God.

The next spiritual weapon is the **breastplate of righteousness.** This breastplate has a vital role because it covers our heart and it represents God's righteousness. God is a jealous God, and we as believers have to operate in righteousness and in justice every day of our lives. Proverbs 4:23 tells us to *"Keep your heart with all diligence, for out of it spring* the issues of life." God's Word talks about the heart alot, so He really wanted us to pay attention to protecting our heart. In the New Living Translation that same scripture states, *"Guard your heart above all else, for it determines the course of your life."* When we wage war against the enemy, we want to wage it in truth and righteousness. We want to ensure there are no holes in that breastplate, and that everything will be intact.

The next weapon I want to examine is "our **feet should be shod with the preparation of the gospel of peace.**" We want to have peace, God's peace because there is nothing better than the peace of God. Philippians 4:6-7 says, *"Be anxious for nothing, but in everything by prayer and supplication, with thanksgiving, let your requests be made known to God; and the peace of God, which surpasses all understanding, will guard your hearts and minds through Christ Jesus."* God's peace must reign and rule over our life and we must guard our hearts and minds. This is why our feet should be shod with the preparation of the gospel of peace.

Our next spiritual weapon is our **shield of faith,** so we may quench every fiery dart of the wicked one. Remember that the shield of faith is very critical because God's Word warns us that weapons will form, but we have a blessed assurance that they will not prosper. So our shield of faith allows us to fight the good fight of faith and quench every attack from the enemy.

The next spiritual weapon is **the helmet of salvation. You** must know your identity in Christ, and you must know who you are in God. Philippians 2:5 reads, *"Let this mind be in you which was also in Christ Jesus."* When we operate with the mind of Christ at all times, the enemy cannot defeat us in our mind when we know who we are in God.

The sword of the spirit which is the Word of God is the next spiritual weapon, and we also use this to fight the enemy. Matthew 4:1 gives us a prime example when it states, *"Then Jesus was led up by the Spirit into the wilderness to be tempted by the devil."* But each time the devil tried to tempt Jesus to operate outside of who He was, Jesus always responded with the Word of God. This is the same way that we must wage war against the enemy with the Word of God, using the sword of the spirit. Jesus always responded with *"it is written"* every time the enemy came to Him. He only responded with the Word, and we must do the same. We can only do it if we have The Word of God in us. The Word of God is our offensive weapon <u>and</u> our defensive at the same time.

Let's talk a moment about the **blood of Jesus**, because you must know that the blood of Jesus is a powerful weapon. God's Word says in Revelation 12:11, *"And they overcame him by the blood of the Lamb, and by the word of their testimony; and they loved not their lives unto the death."* We are also redeemed (bought back) by the blood of Jesus. In 1 Pet 1:18-21, it states *"God paid a ransom to save you from the impossible road to heaven which your fathers tried to take, and the ransom he paid was not mere gold or silver as you very well know. But he paid for you with the precious lifeblood of Christ, the sinless, spotless Lamb of God. God chose him for this purpose long before the world began, but only recently was he brought into public view, in these last days, as a blessing to you.*

Because of this, your trust can be in God who raised Christ from the dead and gave him great glory. Now your faith and hope can rest in him alone. In 1 John 1:7, the scripture lets us know that we are cleansed by the blood of Jesus. *It reads, "But if we walk in the light, as he is in the light, we have fellowship one with another, and the blood of Jesus Christ his Son cleanseth us from **all** sin."*

The **Name of Jesus** is also a weapon, just read Phillipians 2:9-11 which states, *"Therefore God exalted him to the highest place and gave him the name that is above every name, that at the name of Jesus every knee should bow, in heaven and on earth and under the earth, and every tongue acknowledges that Jesus*

Christ is Lord, to the glory of God the Father." So we see that the name of Jesus has power, so we must call on the name of Jesus! Amen.

We must also have a revelation of our <u>spiritual position</u> in Christ, I want to mention this for just a moment. Our spiritual position in Christ ensures that we understand who we are. When you examine Luke 10:19 it reads, *"I have given you authority to trample on snakes and scorpions and to overcome all the power of the enemy; nothing will harm you."* This is who we are in Christ, and the position that Christ has given us. We don't have to be timid, fearful, or afraid of the enemy because Jesus already overcame satan. We must also look at our position that is spoken of in Ephesians 1:5, *"Having predestinated us unto the adoption of children by Jesus Christ to himself, according to the good pleasure of his will."* We have been adopted into the family of God and He is our Father. Amen. We are heirs of God and joint heirs with Jesus, so again, you must know who you are and where God has placed you.

Let's look at 1 John 4:4, it reads *"You, dear children, are from God and have overcome them, because the one who is in you is greater than the one who is in the world."* It is also important to know who the real enemy is so you won't fight against the wrong thing. The real enemy of God is satan, not <u>people,</u> and satan is positioned to try to defeat us, but we know through the scriptures that he is a defeated foe, Amen! This is why we must have the Word on the inside of us and we can discern who is behind everything. The enemy will work <u>through people</u> to try and distract us, or draw us away from the Word of God. We just have to trust God to perform His Word, and He will never let us down. If you are ever in doubt, pray and God will show you that anything which does not line up with His Word or His will is not of God. Ephesians 1:19-23 states, *"and his incomparably great power for us who believe. That power is the same as the mighty strength he exerted when he raised Christ from the dead and seated him at his right hand in the heavenly realms, **far above** all rule and authority, power and dominion, and every name that is invoked, not only in the present age but also in the* *one to come. And God placed all things under his feet and appointed him to be head over everything for the church, which is his body, the fullness of him who fills everything in every way."* Think about that, we are seated in heavenly places with Christ Jesus.

We have been equipped with mighty spiritual weapons, power, and authority to operate in the Kingdom of God. We are spiritual administrators and have delegated authority so we can maintain our dominion that God has given us to walk victoriously in the earth. So wage good warfare, and fight the good fight of faith. Amen.

Chapter 7

Understanding & Praying in The Holy Spirit

Luke 18:1

And he spake a parable unto them to this end, that men ought always to pray, and not to faint:

WHO IS THE HOLY SPIRIT?

There have been entire books written on who the Holy Spirit is, and I know that I will only scratch the surface in this chapter. However, in order to set the tone for this important chapter, I want to start by stating this: The Holy Spirit is a person, not a thing, not something spooky, but a person. He is the third person of the Godhead, and He resides on the inside of every believer. The scriptures in 1 Corinthians 6:19-20 read, *"Do you know that your bodies are temples of the Holy Spirit, who is in you, whom you have received from God? You are not your own, you were bought with a price. Therefore, honor your bodies."* So right there God's Word confirms my initial statement. So often I believe that this is one of the stumbling blocks for believers. They see or hear someone speaking of The Holy Spirit in a way that is unusual or uncomfortable for them. They may become fearful and are not able to tap into this powerful source that God has given to every believer. When you think of The Holy Spirit, think of power, unspeakable P-O-W-E-R, because that is what every believer can experience. Hold that thought for a moment, and we will come back to it.

In 1 John 5:7 it states, *"there are three that bear record in heaven, the Father, the Word, and the Holy Spirit, and these three are one."* There is one God who manifests or reveals Himself in three persons, whom we call the Trinity. God the Father, God the Word, and God the Holy Spirit, now let's look at each manifestation. The

Father is found in John 4:24 where it says, *"God is a spirit and they that worship Him, must worship Him in spirit and in truth."* God the Word is found in John 1:1, *"in the beginning was the Word, and **the Word was with God, and the Word was God**."* They were all together in the beginning because they are all one. When you read John 1:14, it goes on to say that, **"The Word became flesh** *and made his dwelling among us. We have seen his glory, the glory of the one and only Son, who came from the Father, full of grace and truth."* Lastly, God the Spirit is found in John 14:16-18, *"And I will ask the Father, and he will give you another Comforter, that he may abide with you forever.* ***Even the Spirit of truth****; who the world cannot receive, because it seeth him not, neither knoweth him, but ye know him; for he dwelleth with you, and shall be in you. I will not leave you comfortless: I will come to you."*

So we have God the Father, God the Word, and God the Holy Spirit talking about the experience of the indwelling of The Holy Spirit. Now this experience takes place the moment we accept Jesus Christ as our Savior. The Comforter, which is The Holy Spirit, will never leave us, therefore we are never alone or comfortless because He is IN US. The Holy Spirit is also our teacher, just review John 14:25, *"He will teach us all things and bring all things to our remembrance."* It's amazing to know over and over again that no matter what, God is with us and we are never, ever alone. Amen!

The Holy Spirit is also a guide, as an example, there is a passage of scripture I want to highlight in John 16:13-15 which says *"Howbeit when he, the Spirit of truth, is come, he will guide you into all truth: for he shall not speak of himself; but whatsoever he shall hear, that shall he speak: and he will shew you things to come. He shall glorify me: for he shall receive of mine, and shall shew it unto you. All things that the Father hath are mine: therefore said I, that he shall take of mine, and shall shew it unto you.* So we see here that the Holy Spirit, the third person of the Trinity, guides us and he teaches us. He is the one that will show us all things to come.

As another example, in 1 Cor 2:9-16 it says, *"However, as it is written: "What no eye has seen, what no ear has heard, and what no human mind has conceived" the things God has prepared for those who love him—**these are the things God has revealed to us by his Spirit.** The Spirit searches all things, even the deep things of God. For who knows a person's thoughts except their own spirit within them? In the same way no one knows the thoughts of God except the Spirit of God. What we have received is not the spirit of the world, but the Spirit who is from God, so that we may understand what God has freely given us. This is what we speak, not in words taught us by human wisdom but in words taught by the Spirit, explaining spiritual realities with Spirit-taught words. The person without the Spirit does not accept the things that come from the Spirit of God but considers them foolishness, and cannot understand them* *because they are discerned only through the Spirit. The person with the Spirit makes judgments about all things, but such a person is not subject to merely human judgments, for, "Who has known the mind of the Lord so as to instruct him?" But we have the mind of Christ."* We need The Holy Spirit people of God, He is ESSENTIAL!

The book of John 14:16 tells us that *"He will glorify me because it is from me that he will receive what he will make known to you."* The Holy Spirit teaches us all things and glorifies Jesus, causing us to bring glory to Jesus and the Father. So there is an "experience within an experience", and it is called the baptism of the Holy Spirit. This is where the Holy Spirit comes upon you and overshadows you. In Matthew 3:11 it states, "I *baptize you with water for repentance. But after me comes one who is more powerful than I, whose sandals I am not worthy to carry."* This is John prophetically speaking to people concerning Jesus. Luke 24:49 also tells us, *"And, behold, I send the promise of my Father upon you: but tarry ye in the city of Jerusalem, until ye be endued with power from on high."* This is Jesus giving His disciples instructions that He was going to send the promise of the Father upon them. He gave them instructions to go to a certain place in Jerusalem and to remain there until they were endowed with power.

In Acts 1:8, we read that "But ye shall receive *power, after that the Holy Ghost is come upon you: and ye shall be witnesses unto me both in Jerusalem, and in all Judaea, and in Samaria, and unto the uttermost part of the earth."* So we can expect power after the Holy Spirit comes upon you, now I am speaking of the "experience within the experience." We have Him on the inside and we also have the ability to receive the Holy Spirit just as they did in the book of Acts. Let us continue in Acts 2:1-4, *"And when the day of Pentecost was fully come, they were all with one accord in one place. And suddenly there came a sound from heaven as of a rushing mighty wind, and it filled all the house where they were sitting. And there appeared unto them cloven tongues like as of fire, and it sat upon each of them. And they were all filled with the Holy Ghost, and began to speak with other tongues, as the Spirit gave them utterance."* In this scripture we understand that it was not something they were doing on their own, but the Spirit of The Lord began to speak through them. This is available to every believer!

In Mark 16:17 it states, *"And these signs shall follow them that believe; In my name shall they cast out devils; they shall speak with new tongues."* These are outward signs of an inner supernatural experience. If you read on in Acts 19:2-6, it states *"He said unto them, Have ye received the Holy Ghost since ye believed? And they said unto him, We have not so much as heard whether there be any Holy Ghost."* In this scripture Paul had met with a group of believers that have Christ as their savior, but they had not been taught anything about the Holy Spirit. Paul had begun to teach them and give them understanding and revelation about the Word of God.

The scriptures tell us Paul laid hands on them and the Holy Spirit came upon them, and they spoke with new tongues and prophesied. Once they received knowledge and understanding about the Holy Spirit, they were able to receive the Holy Spirit. We cannot receive anything that we don't have knowledge about, but once we receive knowledge and understanding, then we are able now to receive. It has been my experience that a lot of times believers don't have the knowledge or the understanding about the Holy Spirit and have not experienced Him coming upon them, but they have accepted Jesus Christ as their savior. This is because they don't have the knowledge of The Holy Spirit, but once they receive knowledge, they are able to receive the baptism of the Holy Spirit.

In Luke 11:13 it reads, *"If ye then, being evil, know how to give good gifts unto your children: how much more shall your heavenly Father give the Holy Spirit to them that ask him?"* Again, this gift is for every believer and we can receive it simply by first getting the knowledge of it, and then asking the Father for the Holy Spirit, and He will give it to you. You can also read in Joel 2:28 that, *"And it shall come to pass afterward, that I will pour out my spirit upon all flesh; and your sons and your daughters shall prophesy, your old men shall dream dreams, your young men shall see visions:"* God's promise is again emphasized in 1 Sam 10:6, *"And the Spirit of the Lord will come upon thee, and thou shalt prophesy with them, and shalt be turned into another man."* This is basically what happens when the Holy Spirit comes upon an individual, he turns into another person. This is how you can operate on another level when you are led by the Holy Spirit.

WHAT HAPPENS WHEN I PRAY IN MY HEAVENLY LANGUAGE?

When I pray in my heavenly language my spirit man is praying. In 1 Corinthians 14:14-15 we are able to get an understanding of what takes place when we pray in our heavenly language. It reads, *"For if I pray in an unknown tongue, my spirit prayeth, but my understanding is unfruitful. What is it then? I will pray with the spirit, and I will pray with the understanding also: I will sing with the spirit, and I will sing with the understanding also."* You see, when we are praying in our heavenly language, then the Holy Spirit is praying on our behalf. This is why our understanding is not fruitful as to what is being prayed for, but we can ask God and He will give us the understanding. This means we can do both. We can pray with understanding by praying the Word of God. However, we can also pray with our heavenly language, allowing our spirit to pray.

In verses 2-4 of that same chapter, we learned that we are praying to God, not to man, when we are praying in our heavenly language. This is why the scripture says *"our understanding is unfruitful"* because we are not praying to man, and only God understands everything about the Spirit.

Another thing that occurs when we pray in the spirit is explained in 1 Corinthians 14:2, *"For he that speaketh in an unknown tongue speaketh not unto men, but unto God: for no man understandeth him; howbeit in the spirit he speaketh mysteries."* Isn't that amazing! When we pray to God in our heavenly language, only He can understand, we are praying the mysteries of God! There is a gift of interpretation that is referenced in 1 Corinthians 14:27, however without interpretation from God, man is not able to understand the mysteries prayed while praying in the Holy Spirit. In the Message Bible, 1 Corinthians 14:2-3 reads as this, *"Go after a life of love as if your life depended on it—because it does. Give yourselves to the gifts God gives you. Most of all, try to proclaim his truth. If you praise him in the private language of tongues, God understands you but no one else does, for you are sharing intimacies just between you and him. But when you proclaim his truth in everyday speech, you're letting others in on the truth so that they can grow and be strong and experience his presence with you."*

Praying in your heavenly language also creates an atmosphere of intimacy between you and your heavenly Father because God knows and He understands what is being said when you pray. I hope now that the difference between praying in your heavenly language and praying the Word of God in your day-to-day language is more clear. We want to utilize all the gifts that God has given to us. The Word of God tells us in Jude 1:20, "But ye, beloved, building up yourselves on your most holy faith, praying in the Holy Ghost,..." I believe we are building our faith as well as our inner man when we pray in our heavenly language. We are also allowing the spirit to make intercession for us when we pray in our heavenly language, which does not make our adversary happy. People of God, we need our heavenly language!

Romans 8:26 tells us, *"Likewise the Spirit also helpeth our infirmities: for we know not what we should pray for as we ought: but the Spirit itself maketh intercession for us with groanings which cannot be uttered."* The Spirit of God, as I shared earlier, knows all things. So when we don't know what to pray for, we can allow our spirit to pray on our behalf, or pray through us using our heavenly language. Romans 8:27 goes on to say that, *"And he that searcheth the hearts knoweth what is the mind of the Spirit, because he maketh intercession for the saints according to the will of God."* It's important to seek the will of God for our lives.

People of God, it is critical that we not only pray in our day-to-day language, but according to the will of God, and as a gift from God, we should pray in our heavenly language. Now that you have an understanding of the two different languages, if you have not already been filled with the Holy Spirit, I encourage you to seek God to be filled with the Spirit according to Acts 2:4. Amen.

Chapter 8

The Power of Prayer Confessions

Luke 18:1

And he spake a parable unto them to this end, that men ought always to pray, and not to faint:

We know that it is very important to read The Word of God, but it is also vitally important to speak God's Word. His Word tells in Proverbs 18:21 that *"death and life are **in the power of the tongue:** and they that love it shall eat the fruit thereof."* Therefore, it is very imperative that we keep our Words, our speech, and our prayers in agreement with the Word of God.

The Word <u>confession</u> means: a public declaration of your faith or what you believe. As we confess the Word through prayer, we are declaring what we believe God to do in our life and in the lives of others.

The Word is full of scriptures to confirm what I am telling you and I will just list a few. Remember when you declare The Word of God, you are telling God you agree, and you are charging the atmosphere with your faith in His Word. I liken this to being at a restaurant and ordering your dinner. You read the menu, then wait staff will ask you, "what would you like to drink?" "Would that be sweetened or unsweetened Tea?" "Would that steak be medium-rare, or would you like that well-done?" All of these questions are asked, and your answers are very specific for the expected outcome. Our walk with God is the same way! We read God's Word and then you apply it to your life. How do we do that? We speak the Word, we mix it with our faith in God, we respond according to what we are

.

believing, and **we stay in great in expectation** because we know that God will bring it to pass, according to His will for our lives.

Now, do not get me wrong. God is not a magician, Santa Claus, or anything of the sort. But He is a miracle worker, a healer, a way maker, The God of turn-around and Supernatural Breakthrough, Hallelujah! So if God cannot do it, it cannot be done! God paves the way for us through His salvation, that is why He gave us His son Jesus! So when you walk with God, the benefits are a life of everlasting abundance. (John 3:16) Even down to one of the most infamous scriptures regarding salvation, Romans 10:8-9 reads, *"But what saith it? The word is nigh thee, even in thy mouth, and in thy heart: that is, the word of faith, which we preach; That if thou shalt confess with thy mouth the Lord Jesus, and shalt believe in thine heart that God hath raised him from the dead, thou shalt be saved."* The act of salvation requires confession, belief, and your faith. So we must speak these things over our lives to experience the fullness of God and all of His magnificent benefits.

Here are some scriptures to support your confessing of God's Word:

Keep this Book of the Law always on your lips; meditate on it day and night, so that you may be careful to do everything written in it. Then you will be prosperous and successful. (Joshua 1:8)

Man believes with the heart and **with his mouth he confesses or admits** what he believes. (Romans 10:10)

Whosoever shall **call** upon the name of the Lord shall be saved. (Romans 10:13)

If you believe the Word and you are praying the Word; you shall have what the Word says. In Mark 11:24, Jesus states, *"Therefore I say unto you, whatever things you desire, when you pray, believe that you receive them, and you shall have them."* In Isaiah 55:11, God's Word also states that it *"will not return unto him void, but will accomplish what pleases him and prosper where he sends it."* I pray these next pages of prayer confessions will enrich your life and give you a great start with your own prayer confessions.

Chapter 9

Prayer Confessions for Your Life

Luke 18:1

And he spake a parable unto them to this end, that men ought always to pray, and not to faint;

PRAYER OF THANKSGIVING

Psalm 100:4 teaches us to always come into God's presence with **Thanksgiving** and into his courts with praise, **be thankful unto him** and bless his name.

We want to thank him for life, for health, and for strength. For in him we live, and move, and have our being; we are his offspring. (Acts 17:28) He is our maker and creator. we did not create ourselves.

Genesis 1:27 says, So God created man in his own image, in the image of God created he him; male and female created he them. Psalm 92:1 says, it is a good thing to give thanks unto the Lord and to sing praises unto his name. You see, we don't want to try to use God or manipulate God because he will not be used or manipulated by anyone. We want to be people with a grateful Heart, a heart full of gratitude, appreciation and adoration for God and for who He is, for what he has done for us and continues to do for us.

Lamentations 3:22-23 says, It is of the Lord's mercies that we are not consumed, because his compassions fail not, his mercies are new every morning, great is thy faithfulness.

The Lord is **merciful and gracious**, slow to anger, and plenteous in Mercy. (Psalm 103:8)

The Lord is good to all: and his Tender Mercies are over all his works. (Psalm 145:9)

We have a reason to give him thanks, He **daily** loads us with benefits (Psalm 68:19). That means that we are on His mind everyday, matter of fact, the Word of God lets me know that His *eyes run to and fro throughout the whole Earth to show himself strong in the behalf of them whose heart is perfect (mature) toward him.* (2 Chronicle 16:9).

We should bless the Lord at all times, His praises shall continually be in our mouth. In everything give thanks: for this is the will of God in Christ Jesus concerning you. (1Thessalonians 5:18) **Notice,** the scripture states, **in everything** not **for** everything, because **"life happens."** Everything that happens in your life is not the will of God nor is it from God. We can give Him thanks in it, because we know that all things work together **for good** to them that love God, to them who are called according to his purpose. (Romans 8:28)

Jesus said, *The thief comes only to steal, kill, and destroy: but I have come, that they may have life and have it more abundantly.* (John 10:10)

*These things have I spoken unto you, **that in me** you might have peace, in the world you shall have tribulation: but be of good cheer; I have overcome the world.* (John 16:33)

Thanks be unto God who always causes us to Triumph in Christ. (2 Corinthians 2:14)

Philippians 4:6-7 says, *Be careful (anxious) for nothing; but in everything by prayer and supplication with Thanksgiving let your requests be made known unto God. And **The peace of God** which passes all understanding shall keep your hearts and Minds through Christ Jesus.*

Oh give thanks unto the Lord for he is good; his Mercy endures forever. (Psalm 107:1) Rejoice in the Lord ye righteous and give thanks at the remembrance of his holiness. (Psalm 97:12) At midnight I will rise to give thanks unto thee because of thy righteous judgments. (Psalm 119:62)

I will praise the name of God with a song, and will Magnify Him with Thanksgiving. (Psalm 69:30)

Then we thy people and sheep of thy pasture will give thee thanks forever: we will show forth thy praise to all generations. (Psalm 79:13)

Bless the Lord O my soul and all that is within me bless His holy name. Bless the Lord O my soul and forget not all his benefits Who forgives all thine iniquities; who healeth all thy diseases Who redeems thy life from destruction who Crowns thee with lovingkindness and Tender Mercies who satisfies thy mouth with good things; so that thy youth is renewed like the eagle's. (Psalm 103:1-5)

Thanks be to God, which gives us the victory through our Lord Jesus Christ. (1 Corinthians 15:57)

WHO I AM CONFESSION

I can do all things through Christ who strengthens me. I can do all things that God has purposed and designated me to do through Christ who strengthens me.

Jesus is wisdom unto me, I have an anointing from the Holy One, and I know all things. Therefore, I know what to do in every situation on top of every circumstance. The Holy Spirit teaches me all things and guides me into all truth. He brings everything to my remembrance that God has spoken unto me through his Word. I look not at the things that are seen But at the things that are unseen, I called those things that be not as though they already exist I keep my mind on the Lord and he keeps me in perfect peace I am God's workmanship created in Christ Jesus unto good works which God has before ordained that I should walk in them. I walk by faith and not by sight, I live by faith and not by sight I believe and therefore I speak I do not become weary in well-doing because I know I shall reap if I faint not. Thanks be unto God who always causes me to Triumph in Victory.

SCRIPTURE REFERENCES

Philippians 4:13	Ephesians 1:11	1 John 2:20
John 14:26	John 16:13.	2 Corinthians 4:18
Romans 4:17	Isaiah 26:3	Exodus 31:3
Ephesians 2:10	2 Corinthians 5:7	Romans 1:17
2 Corinthians 4:13	Galatians 6:9	2 Corinthians 2:14

I AM AN OVERCOMER

Father, I thank you that Jesus has already overcome the world. Therefore, whosoever is born of God overcomes the world and this is the victory that overcomes the world, even our faith.

I am of God and the greater one Jesus, lives on the inside of me; therefore, I am well able to overcome every obstacle, circumstance, situation, trial, test and everything that will try to block or hinder my progress in God.

I can do all things through Christ who strengthens me.

I am ready for anything and equal to anything through Christ who infuses me with inner strength, confidence, and peace.

No weapon that is formed against me shall prosper.

I overcome evil with good, I bless and curse not, I will let no corrupt communication proceed out of my mouth. I will speak the Word only. My tongue is the pen of a ready writer inscribing the Word of God upon the hearts of the hearers.

The peace of God rules my heart and my mind. Therefore I will not become weary in well-doing because I know in due season I will reap if I faint not.

I am strong in the Lord and in the power of His might. His Word abides in me and I overcome the wicked one by the blood of the Lamb and the word of my testimony.

Thanks be unto God who always causes us (me) to triumph in Christ. I am an overcomer.

SCRIPTURE REFERENCES

John 16:33	1 John 2:13	1 John 2:14
1 John 4:4	1 John 5:4	1 John 4:4
Isaiah 54:17	Matthew 18	Psalm 45:1
Ephesians 4:29	Romans 12:21	Galatians 6:9
Colossians 3:15	2 Corinthians 2:14	Phillipians 4:13
	Revelation 12:11	

CONFESSION FOR SINGLES

I am so grateful and thankful **now**, that God knew me before I was in the belly and His thoughts toward me are thoughts of peace, and not evil, to give me an expected end. (Jeremiah 1:5; 29:11)

I am so grateful and thankful **now**, that I am His workmanship, created in Christ Jesus unto good works, which God hath before ordained that I should walk in them.

I am so grateful and thankful **now**, that He which has begun a good work in me will perform it until the day of Jesus Christ. (Philippians 1:6)

I am so grateful and thankful **now**, that I will fulfill my purpose in the earth and reach my destiny.

Father, I thank you that:

I am fearfully and wonderfully made.

I am loved and accepted by you.

I am chosen, I am royalty. I am holy and peculiar.

I am called out of darkness into your marvelous light

I set my affection on things above, not on things on the earth.

I walk not after the flesh, but after the Spirit.

I mind the things of the Spirit.

I am the head and not the tail, above only and not beneath.

I am an heir of God, and a joint heir with Jesus Christ.

I have the mind of Christ.

I have the hand of the diligent.

I am diligent in business.

I have an excellent Spirit in me.

I am preferred above my competitors.

Father, you are increasing me more and more.

Wealth and Riches are in my house.

I meditate your Word day and night.

I am having good success.

I am prospering as my soul is prospering.

I am healthy, wealthy, and wise.

Sickness and disease are far from me.

The truth of your Word is my shield and buckler.

I am strong in the Lord and in the power of His might.

No weapon formed against me shall prosper

Every tongue that rises against me in judgement thou shall condemn.

SCRIPTURE REFERENCES

Psalm 139:14	Ephesians 1:6	1 Peter 2:9
Colossians 3:2	Romans 8:5	Romans 8:1
Romans 8:17	Deuteronomy 28:13	Proverbs 10:4
Proverbs 12:24	1 Corinthians 2:16	Proverbs 17:27
Proverbs 22:29	Daniel 6:3	Psalm 115:24
Psalm 115:14	Psalm 112:3	Joshua 1:8
Psalm 1:2	3 John 1:2 P	Proverbs 2:10
Proverbs 2:11	Psalm 91:7;10	Psalm 91:4
Ephesians 6:10	Isaiah 54:17	

Fearfully- with great reverence, heart-felt interest, and with respect

Wonderfully- unique and set apart

CONFESSION FOR HUSBANDS & FATHERS

Father, I am so grateful and thankful **now,** for my wife, you said, in Proverbs 18:22, He that finds a wife finds a good thing, and obtains favor of the LORD.

You said, in Ephesians 5:25, Husbands, love your wives, even as Christ also loved the Church, and gave himself for it.

Father, I ask you to help me to love my wife even as Christ loved the Church, and help me to give of myself for her, as Christ gave himself for the Church.

You said, in 1 Peter 3:7, Husbands, dwell with them according to knowledge, giving honor unto the wife, as unto the weaker vessel, and as being heirs together of the grace of life; that my prayers be not hindered.

Father, I ask you to help me to take the time to know and understand my wife that I may live with her according to knowledge and give her the honor she is due, we are heirs together of the grace of life.

I am so grateful and thankful **now,** that I am cleaving unto my wife and we are one flesh.

I am so grateful and thankful **now,** for my children, you said, in Psalm 127:3-5, *Lo, children are an heritage of the LORD: and the fruit of the womb is his reward. As arrows are in the hand of a mighty man; so are children of the youth. Happy is the man that hath his quiver full of them: they shall not be ashamed, but they shall speak with the enemies in the gate.*

I am so grateful and thankful **now,** that all our children are taught of the Lord and great is their peace. (Isaiah 54:13)

I am so grateful and thankful **now**, that I am training my children in the way they should go: and when they are old, they will not depart from it. (Proverbs 22:6)

Father, you said, and thou shall teach them diligently unto thy children, and shall talk of them when thou sit in thou house, and when thou walk by the way, and when thou lie down, and when thou rise up. (Deuteronomy 6:7)

I am so grateful and thankful **now,** that I am walking in integrity and my children are blessed after me. (Proverbs 20:7)

I am so grateful and thankful **now,** that my family dwells together in unity and harmony. (Psalm 133:1)

I am so grateful and thankful **now,** that as for Me and My house we will serve the Lord. (Joshua 24:15)

CONFESSION FOR WIVES & MOTHERS

Father, I am so grateful and thankful **now** for my husband, who loves me as Christ loved the Church and who gives himself for me as Christ gave himself for the Church.

I am so grateful and thankful **now** for my husband, who dwells with me according to knowledge and gives honor unto me, as unto the weaker vessel, we are heirs together of the grace of life.

I am so grateful and thankful **now** that my husband cleaves unto me and we are one flesh. Father, you said, in Ephesians 5:22, Wives, submit yourselves unto your own husbands, as unto the Lord.

Father, I ask you to help me to submit and adapt to my husband as a service unto the Lord. I am so grateful and thankful **now** that I am a virtuous woman and my price is far above rubies. (Proverbs 31:10)

I am so grateful and thankful **now** that the heart of my husband doth safely trust in me, so that he shall have no need of spoil. (Proverbs 31:11)

I am so grateful and thankful **now** that I will do him good and not evil all the days of my life. (Proverbs 31:12)

I am so grateful and thankful **now** that my husband and children call me blessed. (Proverbs 31:28)

I am so grateful and thankful **now** for my children, you said, in Psalm 127:3, children are a heritage of the Lord: and the fruit of the womb is his reward.

I am so grateful and thankful that all our children are taught of the Lord and great are their peace. (Isaiah 54:13)

I am so grateful and thankful **now** that I am training up my children in the way they should go: and when they are old, they will not depart from it. (Proverbs 22:6)

I am so grateful and thankful **now** that I am walking in integrity and my children are blessed after me. (Proverbs 20:7)

I am so grateful and thankful **now** that as for our house we will serve the Lord. (Joshua 24:15)

I am so grateful and thankful **now** that we are subject one to another and are clothed with humility, for God resists the proud and gives grace to the humble. (1 Peter 5:5)

CONFESSION FOR CHILDREN

I am so grateful and thankful **now** that I have Godly parents, that are training me up in the way I should go: and when I am old, I will not depart from it. (Proverbs 22:6)

I am so grateful and thankful **now** to obey my parents in the Lord: for this is right. (Ephesians 6:1)

I am so grateful and thankful **now** to Honor my father and mother; which is the first commandment with promise; that it may be well with me, and I may live long on the earth. (Ephesians 6:2-3)

I am so grateful and thankful **now** that my father does not provoke me to wrath; but brings me up in the nurture and admonition of the Lord. (Ephesians 6:4)

I am so grateful and thankful **now** to obey my parents in all things: for this is well pleasing unto the Lord. (Colossians 3:20)

I am so grateful and thankful **now** to obey all the commands of the Lord my God and to serve Him with all my heart, and with all thy soul. (Deuteronomy 30:2)

I am so grateful and thankful **now** that I am taught of the Lord and great is my peace. (Isaiah 54:13)

I am so grateful and thankful **now** that an excellent Spirit is in me and I am preferred above my counterpart. (Daniel 6:3)

I am so grateful and thankful **now** that I am found ten times better. (Daniel 1:20)

I am so grateful and thankful **now** that I am a person of wisdom, knowledge, understanding, and of an excellent spirit.
(Proverbs 17:27)

PRAYER OF BINDING & LOOSING

In order to exercise the authority in the earth that God has given every believer, we must know three things:

✓ Who we are in Christ
✓ What is our spiritual position in Christ
✓ What power and authority has been given unto us in Christ Jesus

I am the righteousness of God in and through Jesus Christ.

Romans 3:22
This righteousness of God comes through faith in Jesus Christ for all those [Jew or Gentile] who believe [and trust in Him and acknowledge Him as God's Son]. There is no distinction (AMP)

We are seated together with Christ in heavenly places.

Ephesians 2:6
And He raised us up together with Him [when we believed], and seated us with Him in the heavenly places, [because we are] in Christ Jesus (AMP)

Power over all the power of the enemy.

Luke 10:19
*Behold, I give unto you **power** to tread on serpents and scorpions, and **over all the power of the enemy**: and nothing shall by any means hurt you. And I will give unto thee **the keys of the kingdom of***

__heaven__: and whatsoever thou shalt __bind on earth__ shall be bound in

heaven: and whatsoever thou shalt loose __on earth__ shall be loosed in heaven.

Matthew 16:19 *I will give you the keys **(authority)** of the kingdom of heaven; and whatever you bind [forbid, declare to be improper and unlawful] on earth will have [already] been bound in heaven, and whatever you loose [permit, declare lawful] on earth will have [already] been loosed in heaven." (AMP)*

Father, I exercise the blood bought right, power, and authority that you have given me in the name of Jesus; and I bind and bring to no effect every curse, vex, hex, witchcraft, psychic, soulforce that would try to come against me or my family in the name of Jesus. I bind and bring to no effect every demonic attack and every evil force against myself and my family, our mind, our bodies, our health, our home, our automobiles, our finances, and every area of our lives on every side in the name of Jesus.

I bind the spirit of fear, every hindering spirit, every tormenting spirit, deceiving spirit, every spirit of gossip, slander, jealousy, pride, envy, lust, strife, hatred, bitterness, anger, calamity, and every foul spirit of the enemy in the name of Jesus. I render them powerless, having no effect in the name of Jesus.

I cover myself and my family in the blood of Jesus and I decree and declare that no weapon formed against us shall prosper and every tongue that rises up against us shall be condemned in the name of Jesus. I decree and declare that our going out and coming in is blessed. The truth of God's Word is our shield and buckler.

My Inspirations

Luke 18:1

*And he spake a parable unto them to this
end, that men ought always to pray, and not
to faint;*

My Inspirations

My Lineage

To my grandchildren, I am so very proud of you. Continue to believe
the Word of God, for all things are possible to him that believes.
Continue to believe in yourself. Remember to always pray and do not
faint, quit, or throw in the towel. **What is impossible with man IS
POSSIBLE WITH GOD.** Meditate the Word of God day and night,
do accordingly, and you will have good success.
He (God) that promises is faithful.

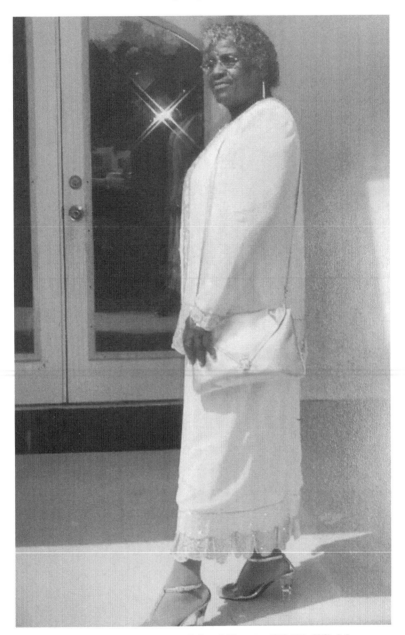

My Loving Mother, Ms. Alberta W. Holifield

Thank you for the many sacrifices you made, and for continuing the legacy grandfather and grandmother started.

"Our Legacy" - My Grandparents

Thank you for your love, your sacrifices, your prayers,
and for your examples.

My Inspirations

Acknowledgements

& Thank Yous

Luke 18:1

And he spake a parable unto them to this end, that men ought always to pray, and not to faint;

First of all, let me say thank you to the love of my life, my Lord and Savior Jesus Christ. I thank you for saving me, delivering me, washing me, cleansing me, and keeping me. Without you Lord, I don't know where I would be! You are my love and my life, and I thank you for being my Rock, my strength, my fortified place, my sustainer, my healer and my provider.

Secondly, I would like to thank my family and loved ones who have impacted and influenced my life, and encouraged me on this journey. **Thank you for a good beginning**. I still remember as a small child the prayers, the encouragement, and the corrections. Thank you to my great grandmothers, Mary Wiggins and Ella Hill. Thanks to my great aunts, Laura Fletcher and Sadie Wynn, who always prayed for the entire family and shared their wisdom with us. My grandfather and my grandmother, Richmond and Delia Wiggins, who always made sure the entire family prayed together. Every Wednesday night we would meet together at our grandparent's house and pray. I remember the big circle in the living room and the room next to it. Thank you for leaving a legacy of prayer, faith, trust, and confidence in God.

Thanks to my mother Alberta Wiggins Holifield for continuing the legacy of Prayer and faith in the ability of God. It is through your continuous prayers and boasting in God's ability that I decided to get to know Jesus for myself. Thank you Auntie Mary

Wiggins Cobb for your continued prayers, support, and encouraging words throughout my journey. You have always kept up with me and how things were going. Thank you to all my aunties, uncles, and cousins: Laura, Candy, Christmas, Lula, Jessie, Leanna, Annie, Sylvester, Richmond Jr., William, George, Susie, and Rebecca for always encouraging me, greeting me with a smile, and supporting me.

Thank you to all of my siblings, John, Bobby, Albert, Priscilla, Mary, Keith, and Shawyna. I appreciate each and everyone of you so much. We grew, we bonded, we learned, and we loved each other through the good and not so good. Thank you for your encouraging words, prayers, support, and your help. I am so proud of each and every one of you. Also, thank you to my God-given Big Sister and accountability partner, Joe Ann.

Thank you to all of my nieces and nephews. I am very proud of the young men and women that you have become. I can not name every relative, so just know that I appreciate each and every one of you, and am so very proud of you. Thank you for every kind word, smile or deed.

Thank you to all of the neighbors, teachers, principals, family, friends and the community that helped to raise and support me. Thank you to the pastors and members of the Palestine

Missionary Baptist Church. Thank you for the Sunday School classes and teachings that I received during the early years of my life.

Thank you to Elder James M Tolbert, Charlene Tolbert, and the New Harvest Outreach Family, my first pastors after finishing high school. **Thank you for another level of faith and maturity in God**. Thank you for preaching the unadulterated Gospel of Jesus Christ. Thank you for your leadership, your teachings, and for believing in me and the abilities that God has placed in me. Thank you for giving me the opportunity to step out in the vocation where God has called me. Thank you to all the Sisters & Brothers in Christ that I had the pleasure of working with in ministry together. What a time of growth, learning and bonding! I appreciate each of you.

Thank you to all of the spiritual mothers who shared their wisdom and knowledge with me along the way: Mother Variesse Tolbert, Mother Shelton, Mother Sewer, Mother Minter.

Thank you to Reverend Lee and Jennifer Fields for being a brook and a fresh spring of water.

And thank you to My Bridge Church Family, **where I am continuing to grow, mature, and expand going from faith to faith** under the leadership of my current Pastor for the last 21 years,

Pastor Vince Allen. Thank you family for all of your love, your support, your help, your encouragement, and your prayers. I love and appreciate each and every one of you.

Last, but not least, A Big Thank You, to Ms.Tammy Wicks and Tidan Publishing LLC for all of your help, support, guidance, encouragement, advice, and suggestions. Thank you for an excellent job.

Acknowledgements & Thank Yous

About The Author

Luke 18:1

*And he spake a parable unto them to this
end, that men ought always to pray, and not
to faint;*

About The Author

ABOUT THE AUTHOR

Delia is the mother of two anointed sons, Jonathan & Christopher Pepper, two phenomenal daughters - in - law, Chelsea & Princess Pepper, and the grandmother of six anointed and talented grandchildren, Serenity, Vanessa, Brandon, Chandler, Sophia, and Daniel Pepper.

I began this journey with the Lord at the age of ten, hungry, eager to learn, and to be just like Jesus. As with all journeys, I experienced many challenges, missed the mark along the way, made some wrong choices, but have never given up on God to help me through it all.. **God is faithful** even when we are not. Delia endeavors to continue to reach the lost through prayer, sharing the Good News of the Gospel and the love of God to those she encounters here and abroad, advancing the Kingdom one person at a time.

Made in the USA
Columbia, SC
28 July 2022

64068763R00065